A practical guide to know

WHO AM I?

*Unique methodology to become
a genius, peaceful and blissful person*

Krishnakumar. P. R

Copyright © 2012 Krishnakumar. P.R

All rights reserved.

ISBN: 1479118176
ISBN-13: 978-1479118175

CONTENTS

1	Introduction	1
2	Brahmam	4
3	Human anatomy	18
4	Single message system (SMS)	26
5	Multiple message system (MMS)	29
6	Solution and conclusion	33

Introduction

This book leads to the realization and changes the perspective towards life. For that, the first step is to understand who you are. It also explains the objects, solution and technique in a simple way to achieve bliss. Learning this is as easy as learning addition.

Sometimes we assume the world is full of issues. Ideological conflicts, terrorism and corruption are the most prevalent. It's affecting people's life in many ways. In addition, various personal problems also exist.

Most of us believe in God and we trust the almighty to mitigate the human sufferings. Thus in the face of a difficult situation leaving the solution to God became a part of our belief system. Whenever we confront difficult situations we tend to believe that our sufferings will be overcome by

    a) God's grace

    b) the people themselves; their muscle or money power

    c) their intellect.

We realize that these solutions are only temporary in nature, as time passes. Therefore, there is an urgent need to reexamine our thinking process and find a permanent solution to this human misery. The first step is to ask who am I?

The search of 'I' may raise more questions.

    Am I God?

    Am I body?

    Am I mind? And so on…

The ultimate aim of this book is to demonstrate the missing knowledge and give solution and the technique to achieve a blissful life. Chapter 1 to 4 illustrates the foundation of knowledge about the objects and chapter 5 explains the solution and demonstrates the technique to achieve it. Every blissful individual will become a peaceful person and a genius. Peaceful individuals can make a peaceful family, peaceful families can make a peaceful society, peaceful societies can make a peaceful nation, and peaceful nations can make peaceful world.

I sincerely hope the readers can take a quiet journey to that peaceful place inside them and enjoy a blissful life.

Chapter 1

Brahmam

Foundation of the knowledge is to know who you are. To know about who you are is to know about space. The great scientists and research institutions are researching on objects in space like stars, planets, galaxies etc. We can get numerous facts about these objects in the modern world. This chapter describes about space and brahmam, its structure, contents and characteristics step by step by using pond as an example.

Step 1: space boundary

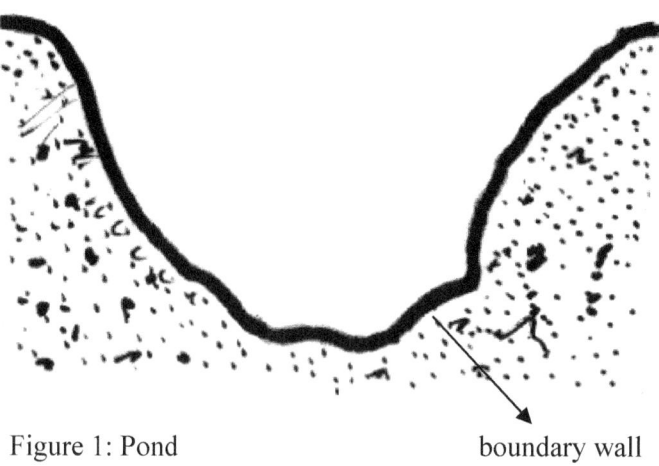

Figure 1: Pond   boundary wall

The figure 1 is a pond without water. Its boundaries are covered with sand or mud and one side is open to air. This pond can take water inside based on the size of the pond.

Figure 2: Space   infinite boundary

Figure 2 shows the space structure and its boundary is infinite and infinite symbol is used to show the symbolic boundary representation of the space. As per the diagram pond has a definite boundary and space has an infinite boundary.

Step 2: Space with Brahmam

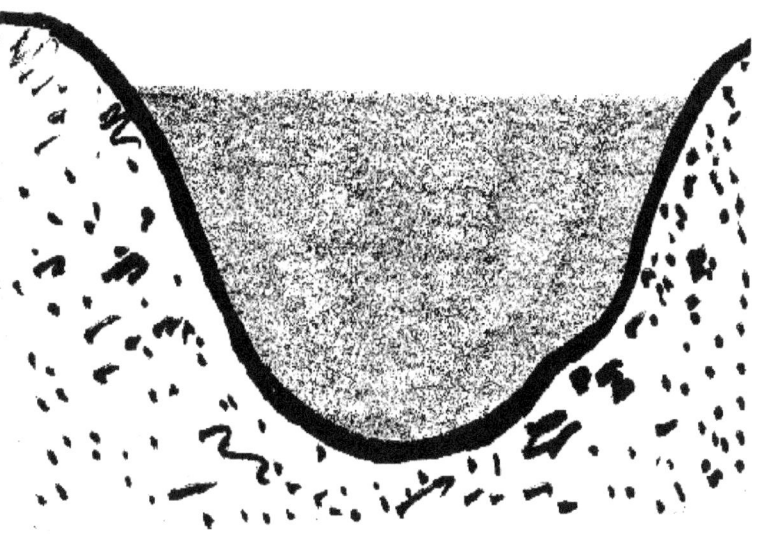

Figure 3: Water

Figure 3 now shows the pond is filled with water.

Figure 4: Brahmam

Figure 4 shows space is filled with Brahmam. Brahmam is an object like water. Brahmam is filled in the space like how water is filled in a pond without leaving a gap.

Step 3: Brahmam's properties

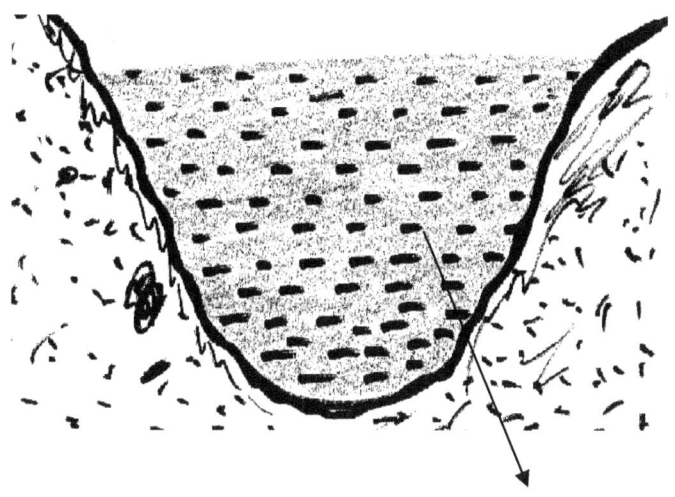

Figure 5: water particles   H2O molecule

In figure 5 dotted lines represent the water body. Water in the pond contains numerous chemicals, minerals etc. But the basic unit of water is H2O and molecular formula is two hydrogen molecules and one oxygen molecule.

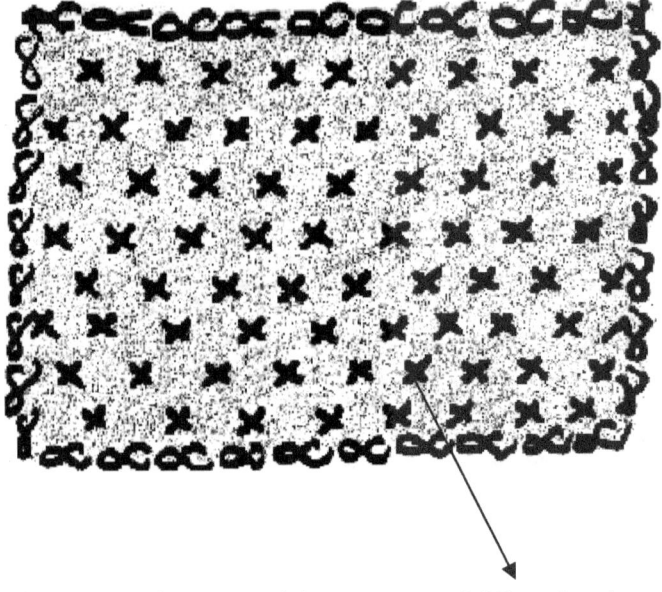

Figure 6: Brahmam particles   x = GOD molecule

Similarly, basic unit of Brahmam is GOD and its chemical molecule is GOD. We have yet to identify Brahmam's molecular formula. This book is using GOD as the molecular formula of brahmam, as shown below.

General properties

Water	Brahmam
Chemical compound(H2O)	Chemical compound(GOD)
Tasteless	tasteless
Odorless	odorless
Universal solvent	Universal solvent
Transparent	transparent

The unique property of each GOD molecule is that it is an energetic particle and works at minutest level of objects. Brahmam uses its energy to push every objects to perform its actions. Brahmam is constantly pushing and moving every living and non living object in the space based on their size and work. Every individual can experience the brahmam's thrust.

Step 4: A container

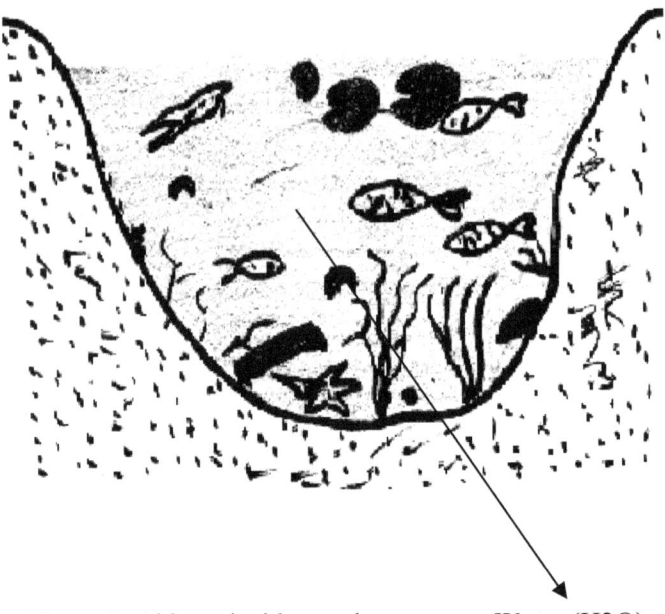

Figure 7: Objects inside pond   Water (H2O)

Figure 7 displays what contains in pond. We can see mud, soil, stones, water plants, fishes and other living beings.

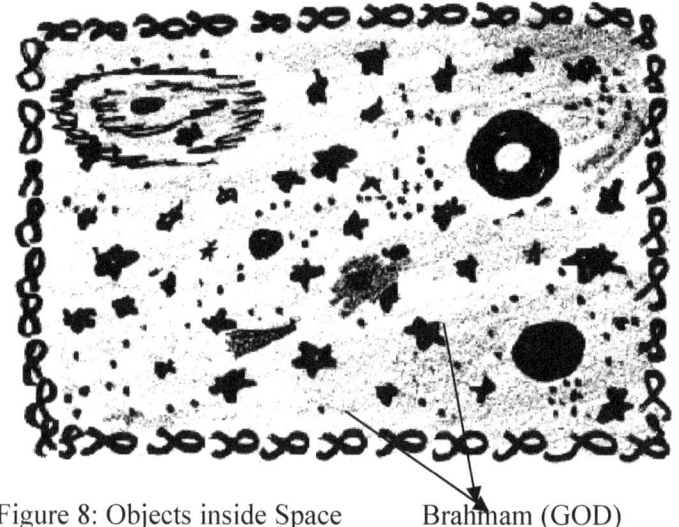

Figure 8: Objects inside Space   Brahmam (GOD)

Figure 8 shows universe, solar systems, galaxies, black holes, stars, planets etc inside the brahmam. All objects are moving inside the brahmam. Figure 8 also shows the vastness of the space and brahmam.

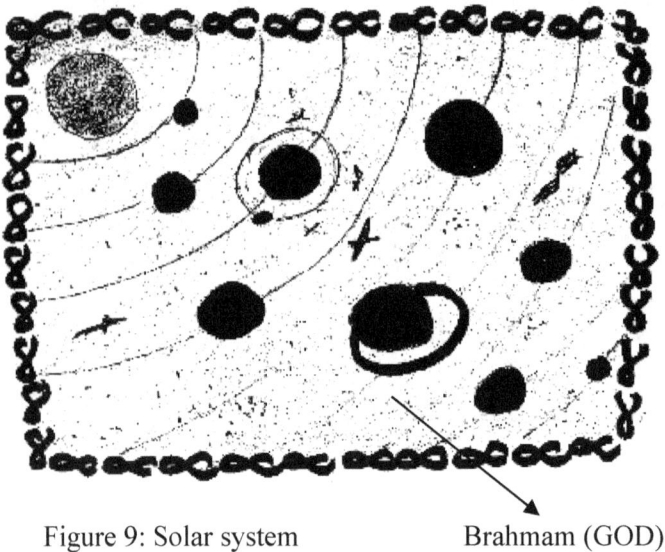

Figure 9: Solar system   Brahmam (GOD)

Figure 9 focuses the solar system. It contains the Sun, planets and other satellites etc. The sun, planets and satellites are inside brahmam.

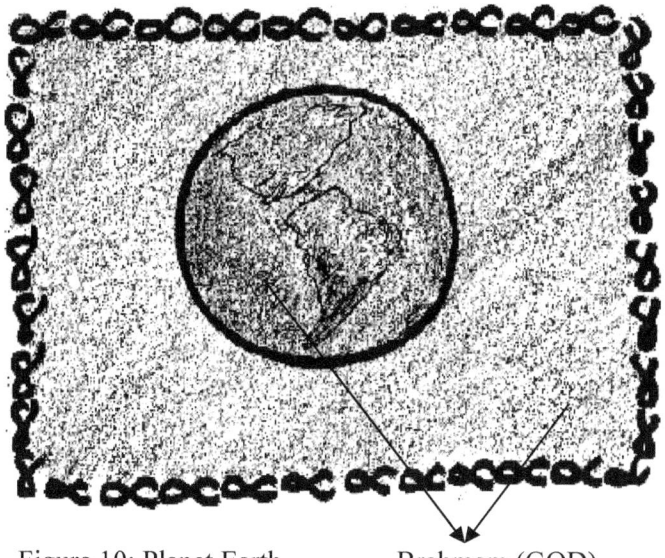

Figure 10: Planet Earth Brahmam (GOD)

Figure 10 focuses the planet earth. The earth is also moving inside brahmam like other space objects. Living beings are formed on the earth by a chemical reaction of GOD, H2O and other chemicals or minerals in favorable conditions.

Living beings were formed on Earth millions of years ago based on favorable conditions. Brahmam is present everywhere in the space.

GOD's constant drive with other suitable chemicals creates life inside brahmam. Brahmam also can form life in other planets when they get favorable conditions.

Brahmam is transparent and invisible to human beings. But you can feel physical presence of brahmam like how you feel presence of water in a pond. All living beings can effortlessly move in brahmam. Human also can experience brahmam's push to perform actions. Humans can neither destroy brahmam nor make a mark on it like how it is impossible to make a mark on water. People can destroy only objects inside the brahmam like plant, trees, animals or other people. Individuals can't harm brahmam by destroying its objects.

Conclusion:

Space is filled with Brahmam. GOD is the smallest molecule of brahmam and base of life. Brahmam pushes every object to move in the space. Each person can experience brahmam's push.

Space = brahmam = GOD = I(yourself)

'I am Brahmam'

Chapter 2

Human anatomy

This chapter gives general awareness of the parts of a human body, systems and functions as second object. It divides as two parts external organs and internal supporting systems.

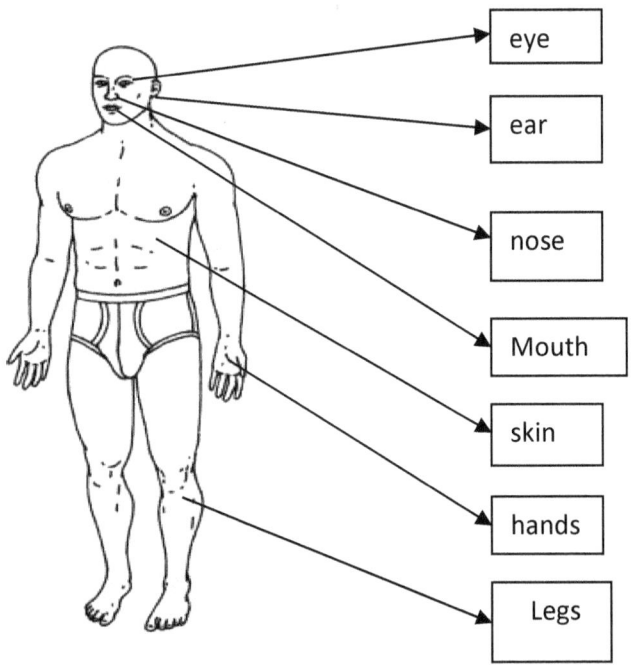

Figure 11: Physical parts of a person's body

The body structure, organs and functions are same for all living beings only type, shape and size are different from others. Firstly, it explains about external organs as below,

Eye : eyes are to see. You can see objects only which is around the body.

Ear : ears are to hear. You can hear the sound only which is around the body.

Nose: The two functions are breathing and smelling. You can smell the smells of substance within a certain limited range.

Mouth and tongue: Mouth and tongue have functions like tasting, eating and speaking. You can taste things only which are inside the mouth. Tasting is a supporting function of eating. individuals can speak to others who are around them or through a medium.

Skin: skin is to sense the touch. You can sense the touch or feel changes in temperature or climate in the immediate environment.

Hands : hands can perform many actions which are around the body, generally human being can perform only one action at a time.

Legs: Legs are moving the body from one place to another place. Human beings can move their body only one direction at a time.

This book refers to the eyes, ears, nose, and skin as receptive organs. These organs are receiving messages or sense the conditions which are around the body. Hands and legs are performing organs. Mouth and tongue are both receptive and performing organs.

Brahmam is pushing the body to perform its actions as a tool by using these receptive and performing organs. External organs of the body acts autonomously to perform brahmam's actions.

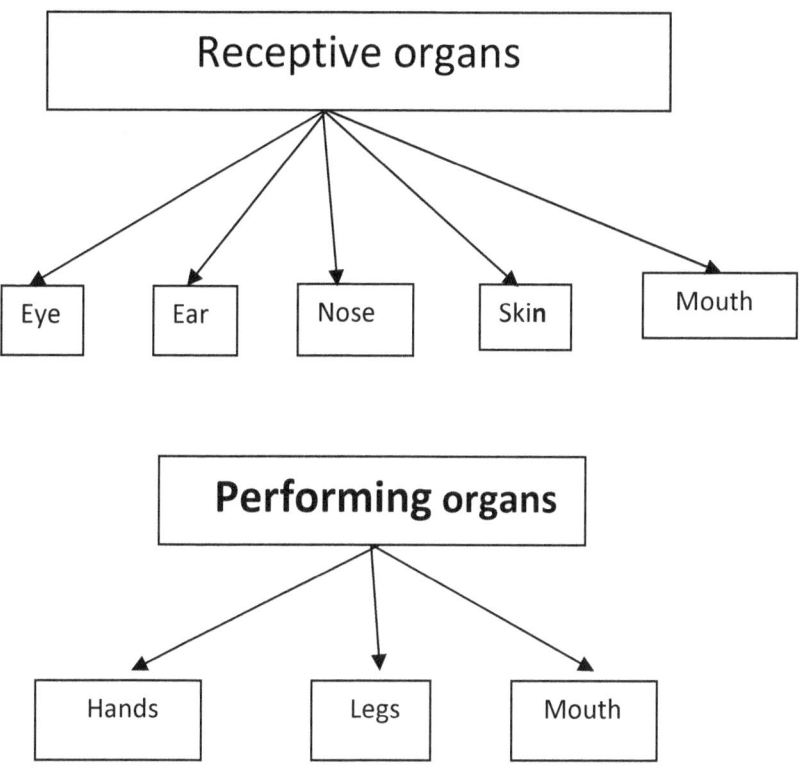

Figure 12: Receptive organs and performing organs

Secondly, it explains about internal supporting systems and its functions. These systems maintain the body to perform brahmam's actions. Internal Supporting systems structure and its complexities are different in human beings and other living beings.

Brain and nervous system function as a communication system to control the body functions. It receives messages through the receptive organs, analyses and performs the actions by using performing organs. Brain locates in the skull and nervous system spreads across the body. Brain is divided into three parts, left brain controls the right side organs, right brain controls left side organs and medulla oblongata controls the autonomic functions and transfers the messages between brain and spinal cord.

Lungs and respiratory system functions to inhale oxygen and gives it to the blood and takes carbon dioxide from the blood and exhale through nose. Breathing is a permanent process throughout life. Brahmam also persistently connects to body cells through respiratory system.

Heart and blood circulation system receives oxygen from respiratory system and food from digestive system and sends to body cells and collects wastes like urea, carbon dioxide from body cells and expels from body.

Stomach and digestive system receives food through mouth and crushing into small pieces, processes it in the stomach and intestines. The processed food is sent to the body cells through blood circulation system.

Kidney and urinary system removes

extra water, waste chemicals like urea from the blood and ejects it from the body.

Reproductive system produces new generation.

Bones and skeletal system has many functions like supporting the body, protecting the vital organs like brain, spinal cord, heart, lungs and other soft cells and helps to move the body.

Muscular system helps smaller movements and large movements. Smaller movements are like pumping of the blood, digestion and large movements like walking, playing, cooking, typing, writing etc. Muscles also protect the vital organs and soft cells.

All internal supporting systems function autonomously within the body. It demands water and food by means of thirst and hunger to maintain itself. Brahmam directs human body to perform a specific work at a particular moment.

Conclusion:

Receptive organs, performing organs and internal supporting systems are acting autonomously to complete brahmam's actions.

<u>Body is the brahmam's tool</u>

Chapter 3

Single message system (SMS)

This chapter describes about a third object mind and single message system. Mind is coordinator of the body. It coordinates various body parts and communicates messages throughout the body to perform brahmam's actions.

SMS is receiving messages through the receptive organs, analyzing messages in brain and sending messages to performing organs. It is a permanent process in the body. Single message system handles one message at a time and it is similar to all living beings.

The brain and nervous system and heart and blood circulation system primarily supports single message system to transmit messages to various parts and systems of body. These systems communication network conveys messages within the body to organize the actions. Heart receives messages from brain to provide sufficient blood to performing organs to perform actions and also carry messages to brain. Single message system coordinates body parts and communicates the message to carry out their work effortlessly at the correct time.

Brain and nervous system follows single message system during an individual's life cycle. SMS independently coordinates receptive organs, performing organs and internal supporting systems. In SMS mind is free to effectively synchronize the brain and body to work at a minutest level. Mind lives within the body and is persistently vigilant to receive the message from Brahmam and this message uninterruptedly flows throughout the body to act. A genius' body follows SMS.

Conclusion:

SMS harmonizes messages between brahmam and body to produce miraculous results.

Mind is coordinator of the body

Chapter 4

Multiple message system (MMS)

Mind coordinates body parts and communicates messages between Brahmam and Body. A distinct thought process system progressively developed within the body as part of human beings evolution. This thought process system creates too many school of thoughts, institutions in human societies based on past experiences. These various learning systems are put into practice in human societies. Human being's began to learn and practice these knowledge systems and messages in their life. Brain and nervous system uses this education and thought process system to analyze the functions. As a result, countless thoughts are passing through inside the body at present. Brain transmits several thoughts and messages within the body at a time. This state of mind here is called as multiple message system or MMS.

Multiple message system is incapable to coordinate or communicate brahmam's message in the body. This incompetence creates conflict between brahmam's push and brain's accumulated knowledge systems and it also adversely reflects in human body in many ways. These feelings and its conflicts constantly burst in human body and makes body restless. These constantly generating pop up thoughts and messages drag human body back from every action. Individuals are repeatedly adding up thoughts into MMS by learning new things. MMS pulls persons back from Brahmam's Push. Push and Pull of these messages inside the body creates nervousness in persons. Such clashes are not only taking away human beings bliss but also make troubles to others.

Brain system's non availability varies in every person based on their overflowing thoughts in MMS. It will reduce the efficiency and effectiveness of every action. These spilled over thoughts not only reduces the brain system's availability but also causes disagreements between these thoughts. Brain is crammed with abundance of messages and commands; it rejects the Brahmam's message or struggles to process such messages. Constant circulation of these troublesome messages inside the body also confuses the physical body parts.

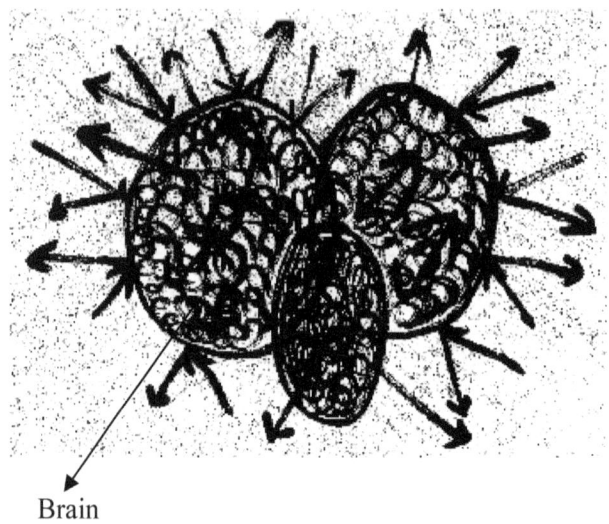

Brain

Figure 13: Messages are functioning in mms

Finally, multiple message system controls body and its parts by applying artificially implanted knowledge systems and hence complicates life.

Conclusion:

Multiple message system or MMS is the root of all problems in the world.

'No one can control either their own mind or other person's mind'.

Chapter 5

Solution and conclusion

This chapter gives the solution and technique to change each Individual's life perspective to live as a genius, peacefully and blissfully. The reason of the chaotic life is the change of single message system to multiple message system. This change is slowly happening in every human beings life cycle. The change from SMS to MMS diminishes the close association of brahmam and body and increases gap between them. No one is responsible for the transformation of SMS to MMS. This deviation was also part of evolution. Each person carries the knowledge and transfers to the next generation.

Key of bliss is shifting from MMS to SMS. Solution is elimination of pop up individual thoughts from the brain system.

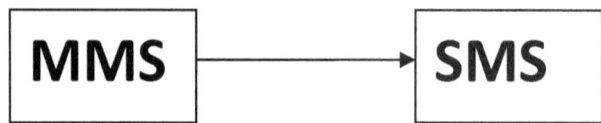

Human beings are doing a series of activities in everyday life: - personal, family and work. When human beings do a single action they receive numerous thoughts in middle of that particular action or actions. As per figure 14, abundant thoughts generate between every human being's actions even at a minute level. This solution can transform a human being to the state of bliss by removing these thoughts.

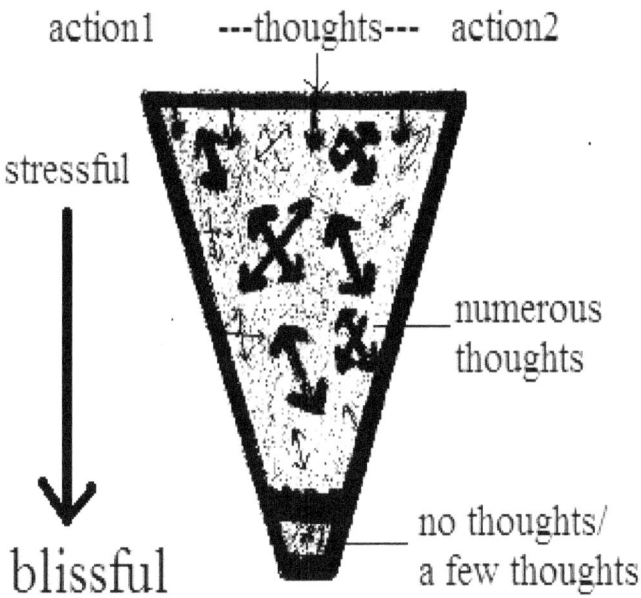

Figure 14: reduction in thoughts

These thoughts can present as positive or negative messages, instructions, commands, orders, people, objects, plans, instances, feelings etc. Some categories of these thoughts are shown below in general pops up in human being.

Fear	Enmity
Jealous	Ego
Anger	Ignorance
Depression, stress	Problems and issues
People	Habits, discipline
Character	Behavior
Corruption	Anti social elements
Commands	Phobias
Racism	Influences
Making plans	Dowry
Restrictions	Results
Orders	Terrorism
Violence	Desires
Greed	Discrimination etc.,

Each one can find several items under the above categories. The list grows every day and intensity of these thoughts is dissimilar in every individual.

Thoughts eradication practice makes mind system to reside within the body to coordinate brahmam's message and body actions. Results are instantaneous based on the depth of the incidents. Brahmam steadily instigates autonomous physical actions in human beings similar to internal supporting systems.

Solution describes step by step as below,

Step 1: Identify the all individual pop up thoughts. Each one can select the most troublesome items in the beginning to obtain the results. The book shows some of the categories to help you to choose items. This book also suggests to choose fear, enmity, ignorance, ego and jealousy are most important items in the beginning. Many sub categories or items of thoughts may contain under main category as an example category fear may contain fear of god, fear of death, fear of dark etc. These items and its force vary in every individual.

Step 2: Removal of thoughts

Everyone has to practice a technique to remove thoughts from the root. Everyone has to remove one thought at a time. It is a continuous practice throughout every one's life. Initially it may take a week, a month or a year to exterminate all listed thoughts and it is absolutely an individual's interest to practice the technique.

Step 3: Mind settles within the body

When a person begins the practice of the technique (explained further in the book) MMS switches towards SMS gradually. Everyone can gain from the practice in time. In a single message system, mind lives inside the body as a coordinator and communicating messages to the body parts.

Step 4: Feel brahmam's push

brahmam   body   mind

Figure 15: Alignment with brahmam, body and mind

When SMS is in place, body feels the brahmam's push to perform actions which is around your body. Brahmam obtains infinite knowledge and energy to budge human beings to perform its autonomous and effortless actions. Each one can experience the benefits, which reflects on your actions. It can be any kind of actions personal, family, work or entertainment. In SMS every human being lives like a genius, peaceful and blissful person.

Technique as per solution step 2

The technique is a simple breathing practice. Anybody can practice this technique from anywhere, anytime and in any posture. This breathing practice has three steps,

Step 1: Exhale and immediately close nostrils by two fingers. While holding breath outside recite 'delete fear' or 'delete ignorance' (examples) mentally as many times as possible, generally five to twelve times based on individuals, but not limited. Construct statements with minimum words to get quicker results. Each one can hold breath based on their capacity and health.

Step 2: Leave your nostrils and inhale long breath and close nostrils by two fingers. While holding breath inside recite the same statement as many times as possible generally three to eight times, but not limited.

Step 3: Release breath and take few long breaths.

Step one to three is one exercise, each person can perform this exercise any number of times in a day. The amount of exercises require for each statement may differ in every person due to their thought's intensity. This is a permanent technique to eliminate thoughts to sustain SMS during a person's life cycle. Let's unfasten brahmam's powerhouse and exploit the infinite knowledge and energy to become a genius and experience peace and bliss. The results visible on every individual who practice the technique are tranquility and delight.

I am brahmam

Body is tool of brahmam

Mind is coordinator of the body

Thank you!

www.ingramcontent.com/pod-product-compliance
Lightning Source LLC
Chambersburg PA
CBHW061519180526
45171CB00001B/255